SCHOLASTIC

READ & RESPOND

Bringing the best books to life in the classroom

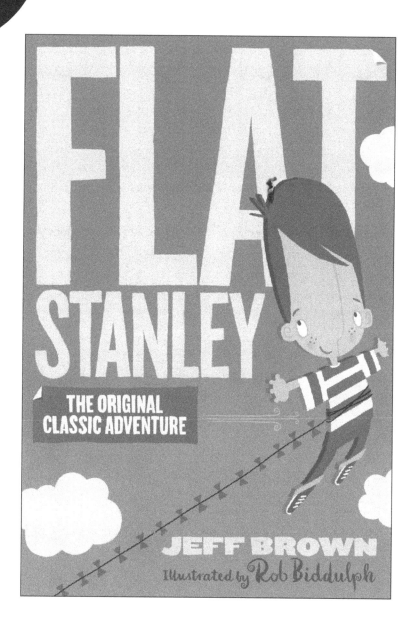

FLAT STANLEY

THE ORIGINAL CLASSIC ADVENTURE

JEFF BROWN

Illustrated by Rob Biddulph

FOR AGES 7–11

Published in the UK by Scholastic Education, 2018
Scholastic Distribution Centre, Bosworth Avenue, Tournament Fields, Warwick, CV34 6UQ
Scholastic Ireland, 89E Lagan Road, Dublin Industrial Estate, Glasnevin, Dublin, D11 HP5F

www.scholastic.co.uk

© 2018 Scholastic

3 4 5 6 7 8 9   2 3 4 5 6 7 8 9 0 1
Printed and bound by Ashford Colour Press

The book is made of materials from well-managed,
FSC®-certified forests and other controlled sources.

A CIP catalogue record for this book is available from the British Library.
ISBN 978-1407-17618-5

Due to the nature of the web, we cannot guarantee the content or links of any site mentioned. We strongly recommend that teachers check websites before using them in the classroom.

Author Eileen Jones
Editorial team Audrey Stokes, Vicki Yates, Julia Roberts, Suzanne Adams
Series designers Neil Salt and Alice Duggan
Designer Alice Duggan
Illustrator Isabel Muñoz/The Bright Agency

Acknowledgements
The publishers gratefully acknowledge permission to reproduce the following copyright material: **Egmont Ltd** for the use of extracts from Flat Stanley by Jeff Brown. Text copyright © 1964 Trust u/w/o Richard Brown a/k/a/ Jeff Brown f/b/o Duncan Brown. Published by Egmont UK Limited and used with permission. And for the use of illustrations and the cover. Illustrations copyright © Rob Biddulph, 2017. Illustrations provided by Egmont Ltd and printed with permission.

Every effort has been made to trace copyright holders for the works reproduced in this book, and the publishers apologise for any inadvertent omissions.

CONTENTS

How to use Read & Respond in your classroom...

Read & Respond provides teaching ideas related to a specific well-loved children's book. Each Read & Respond book is divided into the following sections:

ABOUT THE BOOK AND AUTHOR

Gives you some background information about the book and the author.

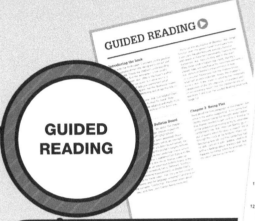

GUIDED READING

Breaks the book down into sections and gives notes for using it with guided reading groups. A bookmark has been provided on page 12 containing comprehension questions. The children can be directed to refer to these as they read.

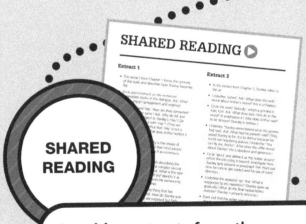

SHARED READING

Provides extracts from the children's book with associated notes for focused work. There is also one non-fiction extract that relates to the children's book.

GRAMMAR, PUNCTUATION & SPELLING

Provides word-level work related to the children's book so you can teach grammar, punctuation and spelling in context.

PLOT, CHARACTER & SETTING

Contains activity ideas focused on the plot, characters and the setting of the story.

TALK ABOUT IT

Has speaking and listening activities related to the children's book. These activities may be based directly on the children's book or be broadly based on the themes and concepts of the story.

GET WRITING

Provides writing activities related to the children's book. These activities may be based directly on the children's book or be broadly based on the themes and concepts of the story.

ASSESSMENT

Contains short activities that will help you assess whether the children have understood concepts and curriculum objectives. They are designed to be informal activities to feed into your planning.

> The titles are great fun to use and cover exactly the range of books that children most want to read. It makes it easy to explore texts fully and ensure the children want to keep on reading more.
>
> **Chris Flanagan, Year 5 Teacher, St Thomas of Canterbury Primary School**

Activities

The activities follow the same format:

- **Objective:** the objective for the lesson. It will be based upon a curriculum objective, but will often be more specific to the focus being covered.

- **What you need:** a list of resources you need to teach the lesson, including printable pages.

- **What to do:** the activity notes.

- **Differentiation:** this is provided where specific and useful differentiation advice can be given to support and/or extend the learning in the activity. Differentiation by providing additional adult support has not been included as this will be at a teacher's discretion based upon specific children's needs and ability, as well as the availability of support.

The activities are numbered for reference within each section and should move through the text sequentially – so you can use the lesson while you are reading the book. Once you have read the book, most of the activities can be used in any order you wish.

CURRICULUM LINKS

Section	Activity	Curriculum objectives
Guided reading		Comprehension: To ask questions to improve their understanding of a text.
Shared reading	1	Comprehension: To draw inferences such as inferring characters' feelings, thoughts and motives from their actions, and justifying inferences with evidence.
	2	Comprehension: To discuss words and phrases that capture the reader's interest and imagination.
	3	Comprehension: To identify how language, structure and presentation contribute to meaning.
	4	Comprehension: To read books that are structured in different ways and to read for a range of purposes.
Grammar, punctuation & spelling	1	Vocabulary, grammar and punctuation: To use...prepositions to express time and cause.
	2	Vocabulary, grammar and punctuation: To revise how to use...the past tense correctly and consistently.
	3	Vocabulary, grammar and punctuation: To use the present perfect form of verbs in contrast to the past tense.
	4	Vocabulary, grammar and punctuation: To use...adverbs...to express time and cause.
	5	Composition: To use and punctuate direct speech.
	6	Composition: To use and punctuate direct speech.
Plot, character & setting	1	Comprehension: To predict what might happen from details stated and implied.
	2	Comprehension: To prepare...playscripts to read aloud and perform, showing understanding through intonation, tone, volume and action.
	3	Comprehension: To ask questions to improve their understanding of a text.
	4	Comprehension: To infer characters' feelings, thoughts and motives from their actions.
	5	Comprehension: To discuss words and phrases that capture the reader's interest and imagination.
	6	Comprehension: To read books that are structured in different ways.
	7	Comprehension: To draw inferences such as inferring characters' feelings, thoughts and motives from their actions, and justifying inferences with evidence.
	8	Comprehension: To identify themes and conventions in a wide range of books.

Section	Activity	Curriculum objectives
Talk about it	1	Spoken language: To give well-structured...narratives for different purposes, including for expressing feelings.
	2	Spoken language: To use spoken language to develop understanding through speculating, hypothesising, imagining and exploring ideas.
	3	Spoken language: To use spoken language to develop understanding through speculating, hypothesising, imagining and exploring ideas.
	4	Spoken language: To participate in discussions...and debates.
	5	Spoken language: To participate in...role play. Comprehension: To infer characters' feelings, thoughts and motives.
	6	Spoken language: To maintain attention and participate actively in collaborative conversations, staying on topic and initiating and responding to comments.
Get writing	1	Vocabulary, grammar & punctuation: To choose pronouns appropriately for clarity and cohesion and to avoid repetition.
	2	Composition: To draft and write non-narrative material, using simple organisational devices.
	3	Composition: To discuss writing similar to that which they are planning to write in order to understand and learn from its structure, vocabulary and grammar.
	4	Composition: To plan their writing by discussing and recording ideas.
	5	Composition: To draft...a narrative, creating settings, characters and plot.
	6	Composition: To compose and rehearse sentences orally.
Assessment	1	Composition: To discuss writing similar to that which they are planning to write in order to learn from its structure, vocabulary and grammar.
	2	Comprehension: To infer characters' feelings, thoughts and motives from their actions.
	3	Composition: To draft and write non-narrative material, using simple organisational devices.
	4	Spoken language: To give well-structured...narratives for different purposes, including for expressing feelings.
	5	Composition: To draft and write by creating settings, characters and plot.
	6	Comprehension: To identify themes...in a wide range of books.

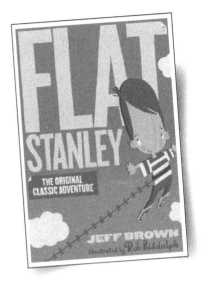

Key facts

Flat Stanley

◉ **Author:**
Jeff Brown

◉ **Original illustrator:**
Jon Mitchell

◉ **First published in Great Britain:**
1968 by Methuen and Co. Ltd

◉ **Did you know?**
Flat Stanley is one of the most successful chapter books ever written. It has been translated into many languages, including French, German, Spanish, Italian and Japanese.

About the book

Flat Stanley is a short book, accessible to all, and ideal for Key Stage 2 study. Exciting, inventive and funny, it is full of adventure and suspense. It also carries serious messages about human relationships.

The main character is Stanley Lambchop, a cheerful boy who has the misfortune to have his bulletin board fall on him during the night. He emerges flat! His parents, at first shocked, are soon proud of his ability to slide through the crack at the bottom of a closed door or between the bars in the grating covering a deep drain to recover Mrs Lambchop's ring.

Stanley's unusual condition provides him with a cheap means of transport to California, when he goes via airmail in an enormous brown-paper envelope. It is only Arthur, his younger brother, who is unhappy. Arthur becomes increasingly jealous when Stanley avoids the unpleasant jostling of people on crowded pavements by being carried by Mr Lambchop as a rolled-up parcel. Angry and desperate for fame similar to Stanley's, Arthur tries in vain to flatten himself with a pile of encyclopaedias.

However, people lose interest in Stanley's flatness and increasingly their respect turns to laughter and taunts. It is Arthur who rescues his brother from his now unwanted condition. His ingenious idea works; Stanley becomes round again and the brothers' relationship is repaired.

About the author

Jeff Brown was born in New York, USA, in 1926. His original name was Richard Chester Brown. When he became a child actor, he changed his name to Jeff Brown because there was already an actor with his name. In New York, Jeff Brown's professional work included radio and stage plays. As an adult, he moved to Hollywood and worked for the film producer Samuel Goldwyn Junior as a story consultant. Brown soon realised that he would prefer to write himself. He sold stories and articles to national newspapers and magazines, working at *The Saturday Evening Post*, *The New Yorker*, *Life* and finally at Warner Books, where he was a senior editor until 1980.

The inspiration for his character Stanley Lambchop came when one of his young sons asked at bedtime what would happen if his large bulletin board fell on him in the night. His father suggested that his son would wake up flat. Some years later, Brown used the idea to write *Flat Stanley*. Many sequels followed and the books have sold nearly a million copies in the United States alone. Jeff Brown wrote his last Stanley adventure in 2003 and died that same year.

GUIDED READING ▶

Introducing the book

Begin with the front cover. Comment on the position and typography of the title, designed to attract and inform quickly. Check the children's understanding of 'flat'. Agree that the description is not usually applied to a person. Ask: *Who is this book's author?* Seek responses to the cover: *Is it attractive? Is it informative? Does it help you understand what Stanley looks like?* Suggest that the illustration makes the book look more interesting and brings the title to life.

Investigate the back cover. Ask: *Is it helpful? Does the blurb encourage you to read the book?* Note that these questions can be adapted and made more specific depending on the edition of the book you are using.

Chapter 1: The Big Bulletin Board

Read the opening chapter. Talk about the chapter's function: to hook the reader. Discuss important 'W' questions (Who? What? Why? Where? When?) Which ones have been answered? Point out characters' introductions (who); an overnight flattening accident with a bulletin board (what); the Lambchops' house and the doctor's surgery (where); an ordinary morning in the Lambchop house (when).

Contrast the author's matter-of-fact style with the strange events he is describing: Stanley wakes up 'cheerfully' under an enormous bulletin board vs the unlikeliness of somebody being flattened; Stanley's unusually extreme measurements vs Doctor Dan's reference to 'these cases'. Ask: *Do you find some of the events and the language amusing?* Comment on the surname, 'Lambchop'; the conversation about 'Hey' and 'Hay'; and Stanley being measured.

Point out the abundance of dialogue. Ask: *What function does the speech have?* Investigate how it can carry the plot forward, provides humour, and reveals a character's personality. Examine the illustrations. Ask: *How do they add to the text?* (They show what is happening, clarify Stanley's altered state, and emphasise his new measurements.) Ask: *Which of Stanley's measurements is now very peculiar?* Make sure that the children know what half an inch looks like. Assess the chapter's success. Ask: *Is the reader hooked by the immediate introduction of the title character, an accident and an extraordinary result?* Ask the children to discuss questions 1 and 2 on the Guided Reading bookmark (page 12).

Chapter 2: Being Flat

Read aloud the first paragraph of this chapter. Ask: *What is the author suggesting? Is he saying that Stanley enjoyed being flat straight away?* Agree that Stanley needed to get used to it. Read as far as the policemen promising to try to remember Mrs Lambchop's rule. Ask: *How can Stanley go in and out of rooms when the door is closed?* (He slides through the crack at the bottom.) Point out 'proud' describing how Mr and Mrs Lambchop feel about his skill; contrast it with 'jealous' used to describe Arthur's feelings about Stanley's skill. Ask: *What happens to Arthur when he attempts to slide under the door?* (He bangs his head.)

Emphasise the seriousness of the loss of Mrs Lambchop's ring: it is her 'favourite' and she 'began to cry'. Comment on Stanley's quick-thinking and resourcefulness. Are the children surprised that Stanley has an extra pair of laces in his pocket? Do they think it is his idea to carry spare laces with him? Point out that Mrs Lambchop and Stanley seem to swap roles during the rescue of the ring: Stanley becomes the 'adult', taking charge and giving instructions ('Lower me'); Mrs Lambchop is the obedient 'child' ('Thank you'). Ask: *Why does the policeman think she is pulling a yo-yo up?* (A yo-yo hangs from a long piece of string.) *What other mistake do the policemen make?* (They talk about catching a cuckoo.) *How does Mrs Lambchop react to the policemen's words?* (She tells them off for speaking before thinking and being rude.) *Why is this adventure with the ring an important point?* Emphasise that it is the first time that being flat has proved really useful.

Read the rest of the chapter (from 'One day' to the end). Point out the enlarged paragraph space before 'One day'. Ask: *Why is it there?* Explain that it divides the ring adventure from the new section of the chapter. Comment on the amusing details in the story of Stanley's trip: having a sandwich and drink inside the envelope; posting him in a letter box; folding the envelope with Stanley inside it; careful markings on the return envelope. Ask: *Are the illustrations helpful? Do they add to the humour?* Explore character development. What does this second adventure reveal about Stanley? (He is confident about going away by himself.) Do the children think he is travelling from England? What suggests that he is already in America? (Mr Lambchop considers a train journey and the American word 'mailed'). Encourage discussion of question 10 on the bookmark.

Chapter 3: Stanley the Kite

Indicate the chapter title and direct the children to question 4 on the bookmark for discussion. Then read as far as 'You're his big brother, after all.' Were the children's predictions correct? Ask: *Why do trips out on a Sunday afternoon become easier for Stanley?* (He is rolled up and carried.) *How does Arthur react to this?* (He is annoyed that he has to walk.) Direct the children to the chapter's second full-page illustration. What emotions are expressed? Point out Stanley's happy grin and Arthur's annoyed, tight-lipped mouth. Ask: *What emotion is suggested by the cold direction of Arthur's eyes?* (He looks jealous of Stanley.) *At what other points in the chapter does he seem jealous?* (When he says 'Phooey' and when he piles books on top of himself.)

Point out the space before the paragraph beginning 'Stanley and Arthur were in the park.' Remind the children of the same structure in the preceding chapter. What do they expect it to mean? Read the remaining part of the chapter. Comment on Stanley's obedience (his parents have asked him to be nice to Arthur) and his kindness in acting as a kite. Ask: *What new characteristic does Stanley reveal?* (He likes showing off.) Ask: *Whose fault is it that Stanley gets stuck in a tree? Should Stanley have stopped flying earlier? Was Arthur bound to get tired?* Suggest that Stanley, the older brother, should have thought more carefully. Do the children think that the author is showing disapproval of showing off? Encourage discussion of question 11 on the bookmark.

Investigate the author's writing style. Ask: *Are his sentences easy to understand?* Agree that their construction is clear and straightforward, but the author often uses interesting and precise vocabulary. Ask the children to discuss question 7 on the bookmark.

Chapter 4: The Museum Thieves

Read the first half of the chapter, as far as 'and Stanley was left alone'. Point out the word 'sneakery'. Would the children use this word? What would they write? (Discuss words that suggest furtive action.) Comment on the image of a light bulb as Stanley gets an idea. Ask: *Do you find the simile effective? Why?* Ask: *Why is Stanley not excited when it is time to put on his disguise?* Comment on Mr Dart's firm 'No'. Ask: *Why does the author describe the shepherdess outfit in such detail? How does he want the reader to react? Is he adding humour to the story?* Pick out the word 'disgusted'. Why is it important? (It sums up Stanley's attitude to his disguise.) Comment on the illustrations and the powerful emotions they convey: the apprehension in Stanley's eyes when he sees the chosen clothes he must wear; the miserable downturned mouth and angry stiff arm as he poses in the frame. Ask the children to examine the chapter's earlier illustrations and to discuss question 5 on the bookmark.

Read the second half of the chapter. Comment on the absence of dialogue in the first part of this section. Ask: *How does dialogue affect the number of paragraphs?* Explain that dialogue requires more paragraphs as a new paragraph is begun whenever someone starts or finishes speaking. Point out 'tireder and tireder'. Ask: *Why didn't the author just say 'tired'?* (To show that it happened gradually and that time was passing slowly.) Ask: *What would sound better?* (more tired) Identify three exclamation marks in this part. *What emotions do they indicate?* (surprise, suspense, excitement and horror) Ask: *What makes Stanley furious when Max looks at his 'picture'?* (He is described as 'a pretty little thing'.) *Why does Max say that they need a rest?* (He assumes that they are imagining a voice because they are tired.) Comment that this chapter is longer than earlier ones. How and why does it differ in structure? (It covers one long, exciting event: there is no need for different sections.) Direct the children to questions 3, 6 and 8 on the bookmark for discussion.

Chapter 5: Arthur's Good Idea

Comment on the change of mood in this chapter. Ask: *Why does Stanley feel less happy with being flat?* (People stop noticing him and other children make fun of his strange size.) Point out Mrs Lambchop's reaction to the other children's remarks ('Shame on them…') and use question 9 on the bookmark for discussion. Consider Brown's development of Arthur's character. Ask: *What new characteristics are revealed?* (his sympathy and his inventiveness) *What does Stanley understand when Arthur holds up the bicycle pump?* Point out the words 'at last' as Stanley delays saying 'Okay'. Suggest that Stanley is concerned about possible danger. Comment on Stanley's gratitude afterwards, the respectful 'shaking of hands' and Arthur's pride at being the one who achieved Stanley's return to normal. Ask: *Does the chapter and the book end well? Why? Do you wonder about Stanley's future?* Let the children discuss question 12 on the bookmark.

Flat Stanley
by Jeff Brown

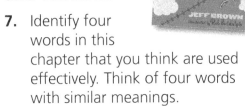

Focus on...
Meaning

1. How does Stanley react to being flat? Does his reaction affect the atmosphere of the story?

2. What are Mr and Mrs Lambchop fussy about? Give examples.

3. Do you think Stanley is enjoying what is happening or is he feeling a different emotion? Give examples to support your opinion.

4. What predictions can you make about what may happen in the story from comments in this chapter or its title?

Focus on...
Organisation

5. What devices does the author use to build up atmosphere and information about the characters and plot?

6. Why does the author divide the story into sections or chapters with headings? Are they effective features?

■SCHOLASTIC
READ & RESPOND
Bringing the best books to life in the classroom

Flat Stanley
by Jeff Brown

Focus on...
Language and features

7. Identify four words in this chapter that you think are used effectively. Think of four words with similar meanings.

8. Do you think the author uses dialogue effectively? Give an example and explain how it adds to the storytelling.

Focus on...
Purpose, viewpoints and effects

9. What point do you think the author is trying to make in this section? Explain why you say this.

10. Do you think Jeff Brown wants the reader to be excited or worried about the things that happen to Stanley? Explain why you think this.

11. Is the author making a serious point here or is he just being light-hearted and funny? Give evidence for your answer.

12. Which character(s) does the author want you to sympathise with? Give examples of why you think that.

■SCHOLASTIC
READ & RESPOND
Bringing the best books to life in the classroom

SHARED READING ▶

Extract 1

- This extract from Chapter 1 forms the opening of the book and describes how Stanley becomes flat.

- Circle and comment on the numerous exclamation marks in the dialogue. Ask: *What do they imply?* (amazement and urgency)

- Circle 'Hey' and 'hay'. How are they connected? (They sound the same.) Ask: *Why do Mr and Mrs Lambchop object to Stanley's 'Hey'? Do they really confuse it with 'Hay'?* (They are cleverly reminding Arthur that 'Hey' is not a polite thing to say.) *What does Arthur replace it with?* ('Excuse me')

- Underline 'cheerfully'. Why is the choice of adverb surprising? Suggest that most people would not speak cheerfully if an enormous board was on top of them.

- Point out the long paragraph describing the bulletin board. Underline the complex second sentence. Circle 'so that'. Ask: *What is this type of phrase? What job does it do?* Identify it as a conjunction, used to extend the sentence by joining one clause to another.

- Comment on the amazing thing that has happened to Stanley. Ask: *How do Stanley and his family react?* (They are surprised but fairly matter-of-fact.) Underline the final two spoken sentences. Ask: *What characteristic do they reveal about Mrs Lambchop?* (In extraordinary circumstances, she remains calm and thinks of practical needs: breakfast and visiting the doctor.)

Extract 2

- In this extract from Chapter 3, Stanley takes to the air.

- Underline 'sighed'. Ask: *What does this verb reveal about Arthur's mood?* (He is unhappy.)

- Circle the word 'Nobody', which is printed in italic font. Ask: *What does italic font do to the word?* (It emphasises it.) *Why does Arthur want to be famous?* (Stanley is famous.)

- Underline 'Stanley remembered what his parents had said'. Ask: *What had his parents said?* (They asked Stanley to be nice to Arthur because he could not help being jealous.) Underline 'You can fly me, Arthur'. *What does this offer reveal about Stanley?* (He is obedient and generous.)

- Circle 'spool' and define it as the holder around which the kite string is wound. Investigate how Stanley gets airborne in paragraph five. Point out how he runs to get started and his use of wind direction.

- Underline the repeated 'up'. Ask: *What is suggested by the repetition?* (Stanley goes up gradually.) *What do the final capital letters indicate?* (Stanley is properly airborne.)

- Point out that the writer now gives more attention to Stanley in the air than to Arthur on the ground. Ask: *What is Arthur's final action?* Underline 'Arthur let out all the string'. Highlight the short paragraph 'Everyone in the park stood still to watch'. Ask: *Why does Brown begin and end a new paragraph here?* (He returns briefly to the description of onlookers on the ground.)

- Underline 'swooped', 'zoomed', 'curved', 'sideslipped' and 'circled' in the last paragraph. Ask: *What feeling do these verbs create?* (a sense of movement and shape) Discuss whether the children feel the description is powerful.

Extract 3

- In this extract from the final chapter, 'Arthur's Good Idea', Stanley returns to normal.

- Underline the second sentence in the first paragraph. Comment that Arthur simply holds the pump and looks at Stanley. Ask: *How can Stanley know what Arthur is silently asking?* Emphasise their mutual understanding.

- Circle 'Okay' in paragraph two. Ask: *What is Stanley agreeing to?* Underline 'at last'. *What does it tell the reader?* (Stanley does not agree immediately.) *What is he probably considering?* (Having a pump used on him might be dangerous or painful.) *What important instruction does Stanley give to Arthur?* Underline 'take it easy'.

- Read aloud the paragraph beginning 'He began to pump…' Point out the importance of verbs in listing the stages of Arthur's work. Underline 'began', 'pump', 'watched', 'pumped'. Ask: *Which other two verbs indicate success?* Underline 'bulged' and 'swell'.

- Read aloud paragraph six. Circle the repeated '*Pop!*' Ask: *Why is it an appropriate word? What does the author expect you to hear?* (The onomatopoeic word sounds like a bursting button.) *What does the repetition tell you?* (The three buttons come off separately.)

- Circle '*whooshing*' near the end of the extract, identifying it as another example of onomatopoeia. Ask: *What sound does it represent?* (air moving into Stanley's right foot) Point out that 'Pop!' and 'whooshing' are in italic font. Why? Suggest that Brown wants the reader to notice, say and listen.

- Focus on Arthur. Point out his leading role in this adventure: he has the idea; he suggests the wiggle signal; he uses the pump; and he thinks of shaking a foot. Ask: *Does Stanley appreciate Arthur's work?* Underline Stanley's final speech.

Extract 4

- This extract, from a non-fiction book about outdoor pastimes, provides information about flying kites.

- Highlight the title. Explain that it indicates what the text is about.

- Underline and read aloud the opening statement. Ask: *What is its purpose?* (It introduces the subject.) Read aloud the next two sentences and discuss the first paragraph's function. Point out that having introduced the topic of kites, the paragraph then answers the questions 'What?' and 'How?'

- Question the children about divisions in the remaining text (paragraphs). Underline the bold words before the paragraphs. Explain that such subheadings are common in information texts. Ask: *What is their purpose?* (They help the reader to find information they are looking for.)

- Circle 'wings', 'tethers', 'pulleys', 'anchors' and 'bridle'. Emphasise that using the correct terms is essential in a text providing scientific information. Ask: *How is the reader expected to understand them?* (The bold font indicates that definitions are available in a glossary.)

- Read the first point under 'Flying conditions' aloud and direct the children to the third chapter of *Flat Stanley*. Ask: *Which environment did Stanley and Arthur use? Was it appropriate for kite-flying?*

- Circle the semi-colon in the final sentence. Identify it as a semicolon: a punctuation mark that can join two sentences about the same topic into one sentence. Ask: *What is the advantage of its use?* (It takes a small letter after it and so emphasises the link in meaning between the two clauses.) Underline 'it' following the semicolon and circle its 'i'.

- Highlight the glossary. Ask: *Is the order of the words random? What is the deciding factor?* (Glossary entries are normally in alphabetical order.)

Extract 1

Breakfast was ready.

'I will go and wake the boys,' Mrs Lambchop said to her husband, George Lambchop. Just then their younger son, Arthur, called from the bedroom he shared with his brother Stanley.

'Hey! Come and look! Hey!'

Mr and Mrs Lambchop were both very much in favour of politeness and careful speech. 'Hay is for horses, Arthur, not people,' Mr Lambchop said as they entered the bedroom. 'Try to remember that.'

'Excuse me,' Arthur said. 'But look!'

He pointed to Stanley's bed. Across it lay the enormous bulletin board that Mr Lambchop had given the boys a Christmas ago, so that they could pin up pictures and messages and maps. It had fallen, during the night, on top of Stanley.

But Stanley was not hurt. If fact he would still have been sleeping if he had not been woken by his brother's shout.

'What's going on here?' he called out cheerfully from beneath the enormous board.

Mr and Mrs Lambchop hurried to lift it from the bed.

'Heavens!' said Mrs Lambchop.

'Gosh!' said Arthur. 'Stanley's flat!'

'As a pancake,' said Mr Lambchop. 'Darndest thing I've ever seen.'

'Let's all have breakfast,' Mrs Lambchop said. 'Then Stanley and I will go and see Doctor Dan and hear what he has to say.'

Extract 2

Arthur sighed. 'Some day,' he said, 'I will have a big kite and I will win a kite-flying contest and be famous like everyone else. *Nobody* knows who I am these days.'

Stanley remembered what his parents had said. He went to a boy whose kite was broken and borrowed a large spool of string.

'You can fly me, Arthur,' he said. 'Come on.'

He attached the string to himself and gave Arthur the spool to hold. He ran lightly across the grass, sideways to get up speed, and then he turned to meet the breeze.

Up, up, up … UP! went Stanley, being a kite.

He knew just how to manage on the gusts of wind. He faced full into the wind if he wanted to rise, and let it take him from behind when he wanted speed. He had only to turn his thin edge to the wind, carefully, a little at a time, so that it did not hold him, and then he would slip gracefully down towards the earth again.

Arthur let out all the string and Stanley soared high above the trees, a beautiful sight in his pale sweater and bright brown trousers, against the pale-blue sky.

Everyone in the park stood still to watch.

Stanley swooped right and then left in long, matched swoops. He held his arms by his sides and zoomed at the ground like a rocket and curved up again towards the sun. He sideslipped and circled, and made figure eights and crosses and a star.

Extract 3

He had found what he wanted – an old bicycle pump. He held it up, and Stanley and he looked at each other.

'Okay,' Stanley said at last. 'But take it easy.' He put the end of the long pump hose in his mouth and clamped his lips tightly about it so that no air could escape.

'I'll go slowly,' Arthur said. 'If it hurts or anything, wiggle your hand at me.'

He began to pump. At first nothing happened except that Stanley's cheeks bulged a bit. Arthur watched his hand, but there was no wiggle signal, so he pumped on. Then, suddenly, Stanley's top half began to swell.

'It's working! It's working!' shouted Arthur, pumping away.

Stanley spread his arms so that the air could get round inside him more easily. He got bigger and bigger. The buttons of his pyjama top burst off – *Pop! Pop! Pop!* A moment more and he was all rounded out: head and body, arms and legs. But not his right foot. That foot stayed flat.

Arthur stopped pumping. It's like trying to do the very last bit of those long balloons,' he said. 'Maybe a shake would help.'

Stanley shook his right foot twice, and with a little *whooshing* sound it swelled out to match the left one. There stood Stanley Lambchop as he used to be, as if he had never been flat at all!

'Thank you, Arthur,' Stanley said. 'Thank you very much.'

Extract 4

Flying kites

A kite is a tethered craft that can fly. It consists of **wings**, **tethers**, **pulleys** and **anchors**. The kite often has a **bridle** to guide the craft's face to the correct angle for the wind to lift it; low pressure above and high pressure below the wings sustain the kite in flight. The wing surfaces react against the air to create lift and drag.

History

Kites are thought to have been invented in China in the 5th Century by the Chinese philosophers Mozi and Lu Ban. By 549 AD, a paper kite was used as a message in a rescue mission. From China, kites were introduced to Cambodia, Thailand, India, Japan, Korea and the western world. They have been flown for recreation, art or other practical purposes, such as communication. Even man-lifting kites have been made.

Flying conditions

Environment: parks, open fields and the beach are ideal places to fly a kite. Power lines, buildings, roads, airports and trees should be avoided.

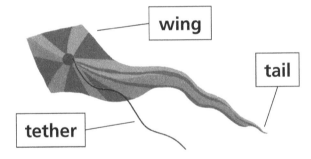

Weather: rain and lightning must be avoided. The electricity in rain clouds can be attracted to wet kite lines. Someone flying a kite in rain or a thunderstorm could suffer an electric shock.

Wind speed: Wind speeds of 5 to 25 mph are the most appropriate. This range works for most kites; it is difficult to achieve flight in winds slower or faster than this.

Glossary

anchors: means of securing the kite to the ground before launching

bridle: device holding the flying line in the correct position

pulleys: grooved parts that allow smooth running of the string

tethers: lines to restrict flight range

wings: supporting parts that affect flight

GRAMMAR, PUNCTUATION & SPELLING ▶

---

1. Helpful prepositions

Objective
To use prepositions to express time and cause.

What you need
Copies of *Flat Stanley*.

What to do
- Use this activity after reading Chapter 2. Read the first two paragraphs of the second chapter aloud. Point out that the second paragraph provides the cause of Stanley's enjoyment of being flat. Point out the word 'by' introducing one cause of his enjoyment and 'through' and 'at' giving more detail.

- Direct the children to the incident with Mrs Lambchop's ring. Ask: *Why is the ring in the shaft?* Point out the words 'fell from her finger' and emphasise the importance of 'from' in providing the direction.

- Identify 'through', 'at' and 'from' as prepositions – words that explain relationship. Explain that a preposition is a word which relates a noun (or pronoun) to other words, often a noun phrase, in the sentence. Prepositions often indicate cause, time, place or direction.

- Write these prepositions on the whiteboard: 'to', 'across', 'during', 'by', 'beneath', 'after', 'with', 'on', 'at', 'despite', 'from', 'for'. Explain they are all used in the bedroom and doctor's surgery settings of the first chapter.

- Put the children into pairs to locate the prepositions, copy the parts of the sentences containing them and to decide if they indicate place, time, cause or direction.

- Share results, discussing the effect of the word on the sentence and why it is a preposition.

Differentiation
Support: Ask children to start with the prepositions of place: 'across', 'beneath', 'on'.

---

2. Past or present?

Objective
To revise how to recognise and use the simple past tense of verbs.

What you need
Copies of *Flat Stanley*.

What to do
- Direct the children to the paragraph beginning 'Stanley swooped right' in the third chapter. Ask: *What type of word is 'swooped'? What tense is it?* Identify 'swooped' as a past tense verb. Explain that tense is another word for time.

- Ask pairs to check the tense of a similar descriptive paragraph (not dialogue) in a story they are reading. Compare results. Suggest that writers usually choose the past tense.

- Ask the children to identify four other past tense verbs in the paragraph beginning 'Stanley swooped right'. Share results. Ask: *What spelling pattern is noticeable?* Explain that adding 'ed' is the regular way to form the simple past tense, but there are many irregular simple past tense forms (such as 'held' and 'made').

- Draw on the whiteboard a chart of 10 lines divided into two columns headed 'present' and 'past'. In the appropriate half of each line, write the pronoun 'I' with either a present tense verb form or a simple past form; leave the other half of the line empty. Use these present tense forms: 'fly', 'sigh', 'meet', 'roll', 'come' and these simple past forms: 'undid', 'thought' 'heard', 'saw', 'worried'.

- Ask the children to copy the chart and to complete the verb pairs of present and simple past tense forms: for example, 'I know' – 'I knew'.

Differentiation
Support: Encourage pairs to check their answers in dictionaries.

Extension: Children add six additional verb pairs to the chart.

3. Perfect verbs

Objective

To use the present perfect form of verbs in contrast to the simple past.

What you need

Copies of *Flat Stanley*, photocopiable page 22 'Perfect verbs'.

What to do

- Remind the children of previous work on past tense verbs in Activity 2. Explain that the past tense has different forms, not just the simple past.

- Direct the children to the description of Stanley's flight in the third chapter and point out the two-word verb 'has… flown' (in 'has ever flown'). Explain that this verb form is called 'the perfect'.

- Compare the use of the two verb forms. Write on the board 'Charlie has gone to the fair'. Suggest that this sentence (perfect form) implies that Charlie is still out. Compare this with 'Charlie went to the fair' (simple past) which implies that Charlie may now be back.

- Explain that the perfect form is made by using the past participle of the verb with a form of the verb 'have' in front of it. Reassure the children that they already know many past participles from their reading and speaking. Point out the example in the second chapter of *Flat Stanley* when the policeman says 'We have caught a cuckoo!' Ask: *Which word is the past participle of 'catch'?* ('caught') *Which two words make up the perfect-tense verb?* ('have caught')

- Give out copies of photocopiable page 22 'Perfect verbs' for the children to complete.

Differentiation

Support: Encourage partners to check their answers by saying them aloud to each other.

Extension: Ask children to create sentences containing the perfect form for the unused past participles in the box.

4. Informative adverbs

Objective

To use adverbs to express time and cause.

What you need

Copies of *Flat Stanley*, photocopiable page 23 'Informative adverbs'.

What to do

- Introduce the term 'adverb'. Define this as a word that adds meaning to the verb. Explain that an adverb often describes how, when or where an action is performed. Point out that they commonly end in 'ly', but there are exceptions (such as 'always', 'often', 'sideways').

- Direct the children to the first two paragraphs in the fourth chapter. Ask partners to find an adverb that is used. Agree on 'ordinarily'. Ask: *Which verb does it add information to?* Point out 'was'. Explain that the adverb is usually positioned close to the verb.

- Put the children into pairs to tell each other two adverbs that might relate to each of these actions: how they dance (for example, 'slowly', 'well'); when they eat ('frequently'); how they walk ('quickly'); where they play ('nearby'); when they shop ('weekly'). Point out that their adverbs do not have to end in 'ly'. Share answers, discussing the information that the adverbs give.

- Give out copies of photocopiable page 23 'Informative adverbs'. Explain that the children must complete the text by adding an adverb to each sentence. The adverbs in the box may be useful or they may choose ones of their own.

Differentiation

Support: Read the adverbs aloud to the children and clarify their meaning.

Extension: Ask children to change the meanings of the sentences by using alternative adverbs.

5. Marking speech

> ### Objective
> To use inverted commas to punctuate direct speech.
>
> ### What you need
> Copies of *Flat Stanley*, photocopiable page 24, 'Marking speech'.

What to do

- Complete this activity after finishing the book. Introduce the term 'inverted commas'. Explain that these are the marks used to show speech within writing. Clarify that inverted commas work in pairs and mark the beginning and end of a piece of speech.

- Direct the children to appropriate pages in the first half of the fifth chapter. Can partners show each other a pair of inverted commas? Which is the first word spoken within each pair? Which is the last?

- Ask: *Do you know the two ways we can write inverted commas?* (double or single) *What has the author used in this book?* (single). Explain that authors simply choose which they prefer to use.

- Give out copies of photocopiable page 24 'Marking speech'. Ask: *What do you notice about the layout of the text?* (The large number of paragraphs.) *Why are there so many paragraphs?* (A new paragraph is started for each speaker.) Read the text aloud, making the spoken words obvious. Ask the children to work individually to insert the missing inverted commas, but no other punctuation. Remind children to place them in front of the first word spoken and after the last. Before adding their inverted commas, ask the children to read each sentence aloud – this will help to make the spoken words more obvious to the children.

- Bring the class back together to discuss and share the correct answers.

> ### Differentiation
> **Support:** Invite the children to work in pairs. Let them listen to the text more than once.
>
> **Extension:** Ask the children to add a few made-up lines of dialogue of their own, placing inverted commas correctly.

6. Punctuating direct speech

> ### Objective
> To use inverted commas and other punctuation to indicate direct speech.
>
> ### What you need
> Copies of *Flat Stanley*, completed copies of photocopiable page 24 'Marking speech'.

What to do

- Use this activity after finishing the book and Activity 5 'Marking speech'. Remind the children that inverted commas indicate speech within writing.

- Direct the children to Stanley's reply to Arthur when he is asked if he is okay early in the fifth chapter. Ask: *Which punctuation mark separates the sentence's spoken and unspoken words?* (a comma) *Is it placed inside or outside the inverted commas?* (inside)

- Explain that spoken and non-spoken words in a sentence are separated by a punctuation mark, usually a comma, question mark, exclamation mark, or full stop.

- Return completed copies of photocopiable page 24 'Marking speech', for children to read in pairs. Suggest that they take turns saying spoken words aloud to each other as they add a question mark, an exclamation mark or a comma using a coloured pen.

- Display an enlarged copy of photocopiable page 24 'Marking speech'. Ask the children to help choose punctuation marks and position them. Does everyone agree? Point out that the choice of punctuation mark may be a matter of writer preference.

> ### Differentiation
> **Support:** Ask the children to underline the spoken words with a coloured pen before they say them to each other. Offer adult support with the use of exclamation marks.
>
> **Extension:** Ask the children to check their additional sentences from their completed photocopiable sheet (see Extension from Activity 5) and add missing punctuation marks.

Perfect verbs

- Choose a past participle to complete each sentence. Then underline the two-word perfect form in the completed sentence.

| flown | stepped | forgotten | rescued | gone | amazed | apologised |
| learned | stood | drunk | left | developed | lost | shouted |

1. Stanley has ———— a new skill.

2. He has ———— to fly like a kite.

3. He has ———— everyone in the park.

4. Arthur has ———— about Stanley.

5. Arthur has ———— Stanley and gone to eat a hot dog.

6. Stanley has ———— into the branches of a tree.

7. Stanley has ———— for help.

8. Arthur and some other boys have ———— Stanley from the tree

9. Arthur has ———— to Stanley for leaving him.

10. Stanley has ———— to bed without speaking to Arthur.

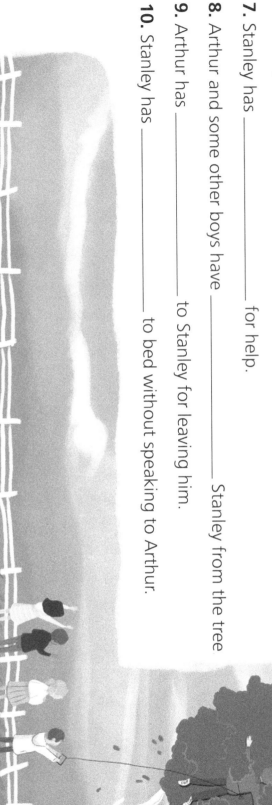

Informative adverbs

- Add an adverb to each sentence. Choose from the box or use one of your own.

suddenly	soon	nearby	gently
later	slowly	arrogantly	carefully
loudly	quietly	suspiciously	everywhere

1. The moon _____ went behind a cloud.

2. _____, the trap door opened.

3. The sneak thieves _____ crept into the hall.

4. The art robbers _____ believed they would never be caught.

5. _____, the thieves put down their lantern.

6. The thieves _____ took the expensive painting off the wall.

7. Luther looked _____ at the shepherdess painting.

8. Mr Dart and the Chief of Police were waiting _____.

9. Stanley shouted _____, 'POLICE! POLICE!'

10. _____, the police rushed into the museum.

11. _____, Stanley got a medal.

- Which of the adverbs in the box at the top of the page answer the questions: how? where? when? Can you complete the table below and add some of your own?

How?	Where?	When?

Marking speech

- Put inverted commas around the words the characters might say about events in the book. Do not put in any other punctuation marks.

1. It was a surprise to see Stanley squashed under the board said Mrs Lambchop.

2. I can't believe I didn't wake up when the bulletin board fell on me exclaimed Stanley.

3. What on earth has happened to you asked Doctor Dan.

4. I love to help people out now I'm flat said Stanley proudly.

5. I felt really worried when we sent Stanley to California admitted Mrs Lambchop.

6. Why do you have books piled on top of you questioned Mr Lambchop.

7. Flying through the air was an amazing feeling explained Stanley.

8. Don't tell my friends that I dressed up as a girl whispered Stanley.

9. We would have got away with it if it wasn't for the sheep girl whispered the sneak thief.

10. Stanley is a hero declared Mr Dart.

11. It really upsets me when they call me skinny cried Stanley.

12. I'm so pleased to have my brother back to normal announced Arthur.

PLOT, CHARACTER & SETTING ▶

1. Making predictions

Objective
To predict what might happen from details stated and implied.

What you need
Copies of *Flat Stanley*, photocopiable page 29 'Making predictions'.

What to do

- Use this activity after reading the first section of the first chapter, as far as 'see Doctor Dan and hear what he has to say'. When posing the questions suggested here, encourage partner discussion before progressing to whole-class exchanges.

- Ask the children to close their copies of *Flat Stanley*. Explain that they have only read the first section of this chapter; there are two more pages left. Comment that this author often divides his chapters into sections by leaving a larger than usual space between paragraphs. He uses these gaps to signify changes in the setting, characters or plot. Ask: *Who has been in the story? What is the setting? What has happened so far in the plot? What is likely to happen next? Where has Mrs Lambchop mentioned going to?* Share information as you progress from partner to class discussion.

- Revise the terms 'setting', 'character' and 'plot'. Ask the children to fill in the first two sections of photocopiable page 29 'Making predictions'.

- Let the children read the rest of the first chapter together. Discuss the progress of the chapter. Ask: *What took you by surprise?* Invite the children to complete the photocopiable sheet.

Differentiation
Extension: Ask children to predict how the story will progress in the second chapter. How will Stanley and his family cope with him being flat?

2. Dramatic events

Objective
To prepare plays to read aloud and perform, showing understanding through intonation, tone, volume and action.

What you need
Copies of *Flat Stanley*.

What to do

- Use this activity after reading the first chapter.

- Show the children an example playscript, examples can be found in the Resource Bank on www.scholastic.co.uk or elsewhere on the internet. Point out important features: clear distinction between characters' names and their words; no speech marks; a new line for a different speech; division into scenes.

- Suggest that this first chapter would make an exciting and funny play. Guide the children in investigating the first chapter. Point out: dialogue that could be used in the play; paragraphs of description to be omitted or replaced by dialogue; characters; and the settings of the kitchen, bedroom and Doctor Dan's surgery.

- Put the children into pairs and create groups of six to share the task of writing the playscript for the first chapter. Partners should write the kitchen, bedroom or surgery scene.

- Allow groups time to rehearse their acting of the play before they perform for the rest of the class. Encourage constructive feedback as you consider the intonation, tone and volume of voices so that the meaning is clear to the audience.

Differentiation
Support: Provide a writing frame and encourage short speeches.

Extension: Remind children that new dialogue must sound natural and appropriate to the character.

PLOT, CHARACTER & SETTING

3. Prompting questions

What to do

- Direct the children to the first page of the third chapter. Ask: *What is the chapter's title? What does this suggest?* (The chapter will be about Stanley being a kite.)

- Guide the children in scanning the first section of the third chapter. Ask: *What questions does it prompt?* Share ideas, suggesting that the reader wonders 'Why is this section included?' and 'When will Stanley be a kite?'

- Progress to the second section of the third chapter. Read aloud from 'He ran lightly across the grass' to 'figure eights and crosses and a star'. Point out the flying details: gaining speed and meeting the breeze for launching; using gusts of wind to control height and speed; creating shapes. Ask: *Is this fiction or fact?* Does the reader wonder if a kite is really flown in this way?

- Ask the children to imagine that they have been asked to write instructions for children of their age about flying a kite. Ask them to write about nine questions that they are going to research the answers to (such as 'What are kites made of?', 'How long must the string be?', 'How much wind does it take?')

- Provide reference books or Internet websites for the children's research. Let the children find the information and write notes in their own words, answering their questions. Keep the children's notes for the activity 'Writing instructions' on page 38.

Differentiation

Support: Ask children to work in pairs to compile a list of five or six questions.

4. Character development

What to do

- Complete this activity after finishing the book.

- Comment that the four main characters, the Lambchops, are introduced early in the book. Help the children to scan the first chapter. Ask: *What do we learn about the Lambchops at this stage?* Put the children into pairs to discuss their early impressions of the family. How would they describe each one? Share ideas and discuss textual evidence.

- Direct the children to the end of the book and scan the fifth chapter together. Point out that by now we know more about the Lambchops. Let partners discuss how characters have changed or developed. Ask: *What new words would describe them in the fifth chapter? What textual evidence is there?* Share ideas.

- Give out photocopiable page 30 'Character development'. Explain that the children must: consider how the characters seem in the first chapter; check the text to remind themselves of characteristics and evidence again; decide on one word to describe each character; and make a reference to the text to support their opinion.

- Ask the children to repeat the task for the fifth chapter.

Differentiation

Support: Provide children with a list of adjectives to choose from. Point out relevant points in the text.

Extension: Ask the children to use their chosen adjectives in a paragraph describing the development of one of the characters over the course of this book.

5. Making an impression

Objective
To discuss words and phrases that capture the reader's interest and imagination.

What you need
Copies of *Flat Stanley*, photocopiable page 31 'Making an impression'.

What to do
- Use this activity after finishing the book.

- Suggest that Jeff Brown often plays with language. Point out the deliberate confusion of words that sound the same but have different meanings: 'Hey' and 'Hay' in the early pages and 'a rest' and 'arrested' when the museum thieves are caught in the fourth chapter. Ask: *What is the effect of these puns?* (They add humour to the story.)

- Comment on Brown's expressive language in the third chapter: 'young feller' and 'Phooey!' Ask: *What impact do these words have on your attitude to the characters involved? Why?*

- Direct the children to the fourth chapter as Stanley poses in the picture frame. Point out Brown's use of italics and his irregular spelling and layout of *'Cr-eee-eee-k'*. Ask what is the effect on the reader here? (The creaking sound is drawn out and emphasised, creating suspense about what will happen next.) Indicate what Stanley shouts while he is in the picture. Ask: *How does Brown express the loud volume?* (large capital letters)

- Distribute photocopiable page 31 'Making an impression'. Encourage the children to re-read descriptions of the characters and their behaviour before they write about the effect of Brown's words on the reader, quoting from or referring to the text.

Differentiation
Support: Encourage oral partner collaboration before writing.

Extension: Expect greater exploration of the text, supported by appropriate quotations.

6. Following structures

Objective
To read books that are structured in different ways.

What you need
Copies of *Flat Stanley*.

What to do
- Do this activity after completing the book.

- Choose a suitable novel written in the first person, for example, *Hetty Feather* by Jacqueline Wilson, and read aloud from the opening pages. Ask: *How does the author refer to Hetty?* ('I') Agree that *Hetty Feather* is written in the first person, the narrator taking the part of Hetty.

- Direct the children to the opening pages of *Flat Stanley*. Ask: *How does the author refer to Stanley?* ('He') Agree that the book is written in the third person, the author being outside the story and referring to all characters by name or as 'he' or 'she'.

- Consider this book's organisation. Ask: *How is the book divided?* (paragraphs and chapters) Direct the children to the first chapter. Point out the unusually large gap between two paragraphs towards the end of the chapter. Ask: *Why has Brown has done this?* Confirm that the gap denotes a change of setting and time.

- Suggest that setting or time could be a useful way to structure the book. The book would have more chapters.

- Ask the children to write a new plan of *Flat Stanley*, with more chapters based on changes of time and setting. Remind them to decide on the chapters' titles and where they start and end.

Differentiation
Support: Support the children in finding extended gaps between paragraphs and changes of time.

Extension: Ask children to name six events in the third chapter of *Flat Stanley* for a partner to allocate to a setting.

7. Changing moods

Objective
To draw inferences such as inferring characters' feelings from their actions and justifying inferences with evidence.

What you need
Copies of *Flat Stanley*.

What to do
- Complete this activity after finishing the book.

- Ask the children to re-read the book's opening two pages. What impression is given of the characters' feelings? Ask: *How does Stanley feel?* (cheerful) Guide the children in scanning the rest of the first chapter. *Do the characters' moods change?* (Mr Lambchop becomes puzzled; Mrs Lambchop becomes concerned about practical details.) Invite the children to write two or three sentences describing the moods the writer creates and how he does this.

- Let the children scan the second chapter. Ask: *What are Stanley's motives in volunteering to go into the shaft?* Share ideas. Confirm his helpfulness. *Could a sense of adventure be a factor? Is Stanley frightened while searching? How does he feel when he finds the ring?* (He is pleased with himself.) Ask the children to write two or three sentences describing the chapter's moods.

- Investigate together the fourth chapter. Ask: *How does the mood change?* Point out Stanley's early helpfulness, but his later regret, embarrassment, fear, fury and pride (as shown in the chapter's final illustration). Ask the children to write two or three sentences describing the changing feelings of Stanley during this chapter.

- Help the children to scan the final chapter. Ask: *Do Stanley's feelings change?* Ask the children to write two or three sentences about Stanley's changing feelings in this chapter.

Differentiation
Support: Expect only one sentence each time and provide starting words.

Extension: Expect greater exploration of the text, supported by appropriate quotations.

8. Behaving correctly

Objective
To identify themes and conventions in a wide range of books.

What you need
Copies of *Flat Stanley*.

What to do
- Suggest that polite behaviour is a strong theme in *Flat Stanley*. Discuss other stories they have read that use politeness as a theme (such as the *Horrid Henry* series, *Mr Good*, *No Manners on Mars* and *Politely Percy*).

- Investigate the first two pages of *Flat Stanley*. Point out the comment 'Mr and Mrs Lambchop were both very much in favour of politeness and careful speech.' Ask: *How does Arthur offend his parents' attitudes?* (He uses the casual 'Hey' to call them.) *How does Arthur correct himself?* (He says 'Excuse me'.)

- Refer the children to the second chapter and the meeting with the policemen. Ask: *What do the policemen do or say that Mrs Lambchop thinks is rude? How do they correct their mistake?* Ask the children to write a paragraph about what is said in this chapter, why Mrs Lambchop thinks it is not polite and what lesson the policemen learn from the conversation.

- Direct the children to Mr Lambchop's encounter with an old friend in the third chapter. Ask them to write a paragraph about what is said that is impolite, and how the rudeness is corrected.

- Ask the children to complete their writing with a paragraph about the rudeness of other children to Stanley in the fifth chapter. Ask: *What do they say or do? Why is it impolite? How should they behave?* Encourage the children to justify their answers with references to the text.

Differentiation
Support: Encourage partner discussions before writing. Offer help with textual references.

Making predictions

● Think about the first part of Chapter 1 and complete each section below.

What has happened so far in the chapter

Setting: _____

_____

Characters: _____

_____

Plot: _____

_____

_____

What I predict will happen in the remaining part of the chapter

Setting: _____

_____

Characters: _____

_____

Plot: _____

_____

_____

What has surprised me

_____

_____

_____

_____

_____

PLOT, CHARACTER & SETTING

Character development

- Write one word to describe each character in Chapter 1. Add a reference from the book as evidence. Then do the same for Chapter 5.

	Chapter 1	Chapter 5
Stanley is…		
Arthur is…		
Mr Lambchop is…		
Mrs Lambchop is…		

Making an impression

● Find each quote in the book and re-read the events. Then write your answers in the boxes.

	How do you react to these words? Why?	How do you feel about the character? Why?
'I am not playing with a yo-yo!' Mrs Lambchop said sharply.		
'As a pancake,' said Mr Lambchop. 'Darndest thing I've ever seen.'		
'Put some more on me,' Arthur said when he saw them. 'Don't just stand there. Help me.'		
Stanley shook his right foot twice, and with a little whooshing sound it swelled out to match the left one.		

TALK ABOUT IT ▶

1. What a story!

Objective
To give well-structured narratives for different purposes, including for expressing feelings.

What you need
Copies of *Flat Stanley*, photocopiable page 35 'What a story!'

What to do
- Point out that Chapter 1 ends after an unusual day for everyone. Point out the ordinary beginning to the parents' day; Arthur's confusion; the position of the bulletin board; Stanley's sleeping ignorance; the shock when the board is lifted up; Mrs Lambchop's practical planning; Doctor Dan's calm diagnosis.

- Explain that the children are going to tell the story of the first chapter from one character's point of view. Ask them to decide which character to be: Stanley, Arthur, Mr Lambchop or Mrs Lambchop. Explain that, as storytellers, they must organise their facts in order, describe their feelings and include details, perhaps with information or memories known only to them.

- Give the children photocopiable page 35 'What a story!' and ask them to make notes to remind them what happened. Emphasise that they will be telling, not reading, their story. If appropriate, the boxes can be cut out of the photocopiable sheet and used as cue cards.

- Let the children practise their storytelling with a partner. Organise storytelling groups, so that everyone experiences speaking to a group.

Differentiation
Support: Ask the children to do one-word notes for a reduced number of cue cards.

Extension: Ask children to take the role of Doctor Dan or the nurse.

2. Frozen moments

Objective
To use spoken language to develop understanding.

What you need
Copies of *Flat Stanley*, cut-out cards from photocopiable page 36 'Frozen moments'.

What to do
- Use this activity after reading the second chapter. Explain or revise the term 'freeze-frame': children take on the roles of story characters and create a still picture of a particular moment in the story.

- Arrange the children in groups of four. Give each group one of the cards from photocopiable page 36 'Frozen moments'. Ask them to work out a freeze-frame for that story moment, without looking at the book. Allow five to ten minutes for discussion and rehearsal, encouraging every member of the group to contribute to decision making.

- Let each group present their freeze-frame to the class. Can the class identify the story moment? Do they recognise the characters? Select individual characters to step out of the tableau and say what they are thinking.

- For other characters in the tableau, encourage the audience to consider what they seem to be thinking. Use 'thought tracking', when an audience member stands next to that character and speaks their thoughts aloud.

- Talk about the relevance of facial expression and body language in freeze-frames. Ask the class: *Which expressions and body language helped you for thought tracking? How?*

Differentiation
Support: Move among groups, offering suggestions for poses.

Extension: Ask children to plan alternative freeze-frames that will suggest different feelings.

3. Listen to your conscience

Objective

To use spoken language to develop understanding through speculating, hypothesising, imagining and exploring ideas.

What you need

Copies of *Flat Stanley*.

Cross-curricular link

Drama

What to do

- Use this activity after reading the third chapter.

- Suggest that Stanley has a mixture of good and bad characteristics: sometimes thinking about others, sometimes selfish. Point out, in the second chapter, his generosity when he volunteers to look for his mother's ring, and later, in the third chapter, his sulky refusal to speak to Arthur at bedtime.

- Divide the class into two groups: Group A represents Stanley's good side, Group B represents his bad side. Ask Group A to think of comments to persuade Stanley to accept Arthur's apology and to talk to him. Ask Group B to think of comments to encourage him to ignore Arthur.

- Organise the two groups into parallel lines facing each other. Take the role of Stanley and walk down the 'alley' between the lines. As you reach each child, nod to them to speak their comments. At the end of the alley, make your decision.

- Choose some children to act as Stanley and repeat the conscience alley. Does each Stanley reach the same decision?

- Try the activity with other situations from the first three chapters. Create smaller conscience alleys so that more children experience listening to their conscience.

Differentiation

Support: Let children consult with a partner before speaking in the conscience alley activity.

Extension: Ask children to plan a conscience alley situation for Arthur, Mrs Lambchop or one of the policemen.

4. Stop or proceed?

Objective

To participate in discussions and debates.

What you need

Copies of *Flat Stanley*, photocopiable page 37 'Stop or proceed?'

What to do

- Complete this activity after finishing the book.

- Direct the children to where Arthur says 'Aha!' and holds up a bicycle pump in the final chapter. Point out the silent discussion as he and Stanley look at each other and think about using the pump; indicate Stanley's 'Okay'. Explain that you want the children to consider whether Stanley should have rejected Arthur's idea at this point or carried on.

- Put the children into pairs with a copy of photocopiable page 37 'Stop or proceed?' Encourage partner and class discussion of the statements on the sheet.

- Ask partners to discuss and decide which side to support. (Ensure there are children supporting both sides.) The children must choose the statements to support their case. Suggest writing notes that list two or three new arguments; the children may like to consider points such as safety, behaviour and parental responsibility.

- Give yourself the role of chairing the debate and listening to arguments from both sides. Allow everyone to speak.

- Finally, sum up. Do some children want to change their minds? Ask them to make their final decision and vote.

Differentiation

Support: Suggest children read out the statement that they think is the most effective argument.

Extension: Ask them to argue a third way: persuading Mr and Mrs Lambchop to work with them.

5. In the hot-seat

Objective
To participate in role play and to infer characters' feelings, thoughts and motives.

What you need
Copies of *Flat Stanley*.

Cross-curricular link
Drama

What to do
- Use this activity after finishing the book.

- Suggest that the reader sometimes wants more detail about characters' feelings and motives than is given explicitly in the text. For example: are Mr and Mrs Lambchop worried about Stanley's future as a flat person? How frightened is Stanley when Arthur uses the pump?

- Focus on Stanley's experiences in the museum. Ask the children, after partner discussion, to agree on and write two questions they would like to ask him (perhaps about why he agreed to be in the painting, what he expected, how he felt at different times). Ask groups of four to compare questions and to agree on two group questions.

- Explain the term 'hot-seat', which means a role play in which a character is interviewed. Put yourself in the hot-seat as Stanley. Turn away and try to make a change to your appearance. Turn and face the class, and invite the groups to ask you their questions, making sure that you answer in role.

- Let groups discuss what they found out about Stanley's personality, feelings and motivation. Compare findings as a class.

- Select a different character at another key point in the story. Repeat the task as a group activity, one group member taking the hot-seat to answer the others' questions.

Differentiation
Support: Provide the children with question starters.

Extension: Ask the children to make close references to the text.

6. Being flat

Objective
To maintain attention and participate actively in collaborative conversations, staying on topic and initiating and responding to comments.

What you need
Copies of *Flat Stanley*.

What to do
- Use this activity after finishing the book. Ask: *Who is the main character? What is special about him?* Point out that Stanley's flat state is emphasised by being part of the title.

- Explain that the children are going to explore the importance of Stanley's flatness in this story. Help them to scan the first chapter. Put them into pairs to discuss how Stanley feels about his flatness at this stage. Encourage them to make brief notes on their views.

- Ask the children to scan the second chapter and encourage pairs to consider: *How is Stanley affected by being flat? What benefits are there?* Let the children discuss and make brief notes.

- Ask pairs to investigate Stanley's enjoyment of his flat state in the third chapter and the use he makes of it in the fourth chapter. Follow the same format of scanning, partner discussion and note-making.

- When the children have scanned the fifth chapter, ask: *What effect does being flat have on Stanley here? Is he still cheerful about it?* After partner discussion let the children make their own brief notes.

- Share results in group discussions, asking for an oral contribution from everyone. Can the class reach some final conclusions on how Stanley feels about being different.

Differentiation
Support: Give the children a sentence opener when speaking.

Extension: Form new discussion groups, in which children express a wider range of views.

What a story!

● Write notes to complete the questions below and use them to help you tell the first chapter of the story from the point of view of one of the Lambchops.

1. Who are you? _____

What were you doing first thing this morning?

_____

_____

2. What did you think when you saw the board had fallen down?

_____

_____

Were you worried about Stanley/yourself?

_____

_____

3. How did you feel when you saw Stanley/yourself in this new, flat state?

_____

_____

Were you upset? _____

_____

4. Did anything surprise you about the visit to the doctor?

_____

_____

5. What are you thinking and feeling at the end of the chapter?

_____

_____

_____

Frozen moments

- Read your part of the story with your group.

- Create a freeze-frame of the scene.

Mr and Mrs Lambchop are lifting a large notice board off Stanley. Stanley is cheerful but flat. Mr and Mrs Lambchop and Arthur stare at him with shocked expressions. 	Mr and Mrs Lambchop are posting Stanley in a large envelope. Mr Lambchop is handing Stanley a carton of milk; Mrs Lambchop gives him an egg-salad sandwich. Arthur is nearby, looking jealous.
Dr Dan watches as his nurse measures Stanley. Stanley stands very still and the nurse calls out the measurements. Mrs Lambchop writes them down. 	Mr Lambchop is talking to a friend in the street. Mr Lambchop holds Arthur's hand; in his other hand, he holds a loop of string attached to a rolled-up Stanley. Stanley is pleased that he does not have to walk; Arthur is looking at Stanley, jealously.
Mrs Lambchop is kneeling on the ground, pulling on a lace. She is pulling Stanley up between the bars of a grating. He is holding a ring and looks very pleased. Two policeman stand nearby looking surprised and puzzled.	In the park, Stanley has become a kite and Arthur is flying him. Two other children point up at Stanley and watch admiringly.
Mrs Lambchop and Stanley are standing on the pavement. Stanley proudly holds his mother's ring in his hand. Mrs Lambchop is telling two policemen off for making rude remarks about Stanley and her. The policemen look apologetic.	In the park, Arthur has become tired of flying Stanley. He is wedging the spool in the fork of a tree. Arthur is looking towards two boys who are eating hot dogs. They are waving to Arthur to come and join them.

Stop or proceed?

● Read the statements below. Do you want Stanley to agree to the pump being used or to refuse? Tick the statements which support your case.

I think Stanley should:

☐ agree to Arthur's offer.

☐ refuse the offer.

Statements that support my opinion are:

☐ Stanley could return to normal if Arthur inflates him.

☐ There are advantages to being flat.

☐ The pump is old and has not been used recently.

☐ Stanley could get hurt.

☐ Arthur is too young to know what he is doing.

☐ It is worth a try because they can always stop if it hurts.

☐ They have agreed on only a small hand signal for stopping.

☐ Arthur may be hoping that his idea will make him famous.

● Think of your own statements to support your argument.

_____

_____

_____

_____

_____

_____

_____

_____

GET WRITING ▶

1. A point of view...

Objective
To choose pronouns appropriately for clarity and cohesion and to avoid repetition.

What you need
Copies of *Flat Stanley*.

What to do

- Re-read the third chapter's first two pages. Ask: *Which narrative form is used, third or first person?* (third person) *How can you tell?* ('They', 'them' 'he' and 'him' are used.) Explain that the author has written the book from the point of view of an outsider.

- Examine the paragraph beginning 'Mr Lambchop discovered that he could roll Stanley up without hurting him...' Ask: *Who is meant by 'him'?* (Stanley) *Why doesn't the author write 'Stanley'?* (to avoid repetition) Read aloud the first two sentences of the paragraph, substituting names for the pronouns to demonstrate how repetitive and ambiguous the writing sounds.

- Scan the second half of the chapter together and discuss what happens when Stanley and Arthur are in the park. Investigate how their feelings change. Ask: *What happens as Stanley flies longer? How do the two characters feel?* (Stanley enjoys showing off; Arthur is bored.) *How do they feel afterwards?* (Stanley is cross; Arthur is sorry.)

- Suggest that it would be interesting to follow the park incident from one brother's point of view. Ask: *What pronouns would be used?* ('I' and 'me') Ask the children to write Arthur's account of what happened when he was flying Stanley. Remind them to be careful with pronouns, making sure it is clear who performs an action, while not repeating names too often.

Differentiation
Extension: Ask children to write Stanley's account of events as well, and then compare their two narratives.

2. Writing instructions

Objective
To draft and write non-narrative material, using simple organisational devices.

What you need
Copies of *Flat Stanley*, children's notes from activity 'Prompting questions' on page 26.

Cross-curricular link
Science

What to do

- Use this activity after reading the third chapter and doing the activity 'Prompting questions' on page 26. Remind the children of the notes they made in preparation for writing a set of children's instructions for flying a kite.

- Revise the main features of instructions: a title stating what the instructions are for; a list of the equipment needed; clear, short sentences on separate lines; easy to understand language; present tense verbs; imperative (command) verbs; chronological order; numbers or letters to emphasise the order; time words (for example 'next'); helpful illustrations or diagrams; organisational devices such as bullet points and headings.

- Return the children's notes from the activity 'Prompting questions' on page 26. Ask the children to decide on their title and write a draft version of their instructions, using their notes to inform the content of their instructions, but writing full sentences. When finished, suggest that the children check, correct, proofread, edit and improve, before producing a final version.

Differentiation
Support: Suggest a title and headings and guide children with the layout.

3. Book review

Objective
To discuss writing similar to that which they are planning to write in order to learn from its structure, vocabulary and grammar.

What you need
Copies of *Flat Stanley*, photocopiable page 41 'Book review'.

What to do
- Use this activity after finishing the book.

- Ask the children to tell a partner what a book review is. Share ideas and ask: *What are reviews for? Who writes them? Where are they published? Who reads them?*

- Read or display example book reviews, such as those in the Resource Bank on the Scholastic website www.scholastic.co.uk. Explain that there is no set format. Talk about common features: book title, author and, if appropriate, illustrator; story information (without revealing too much of the plot); personal likes or dislikes of parts of the book; a comment about its suitability for others.

- Hold a class discussion in which the children express their opinions of Flat Stanley. Emphasise that their views are not right or wrong: tastes are personal. However, encourage them to support their views with reference to the book. Ask: *What did you particularly enjoy about the book? Where did you think it was most and least successful?*

- Give out photocopiable page 41 'Book review' for the children to write a book review of Flat Stanley. Ask for whole sentences in most sections.

Differentiation
Support: Offer suggestions and encourage partner discussion when children are deciding what they most liked or disliked about *Flat Stanley*.

Extension: Let the children use their completed photocopiable as a plan to help them write a polished review for a magazine or website.

4. Becoming famous

Objective
To plan their writing by discussing and recording ideas.

What you need
Copies of *Flat Stanley*, photocopiable page 42 'Becoming famous'.

What to do
- Complete this activity after finishing the book.

- Ask: *Do you think the writer planned the ending before he started writing the story? Why does planning beforehand improve a story?* Agree that the writer is able to build up to the ending.

- Suggest that Arthur's feelings are very important in this story. Remind the children of Arthur's jealous attempts to squeeze under a door in the second chapter and to flatten himself with books in the third chapter. Direct the children to Arthur's speech about fame in the third chapter ('Some day…') and read it aloud. Point out that it is not being flat that Arthur is jealous of, it is being famous and also discuss how, although this story has a happy ending, Brown does not fulfil Arthur's wish.

- Suggest writing a short sixth chapter in which Stanley is back to normal and Arthur becomes famous. Give out individual copies of photocopiable page 42 'Becoming famous' for the children to make planning notes for their sixth chapter. Let partners discuss their completed plans before, independently, writing their own endings.

- Invite some children to share their endings. Evaluate them as a class, to see if they fit in with the author's style and meet Arthur's aims.

Differentiation
Support: Suggest the children draw pictures of their ending and write short sentences to accompany each picture.

Extension: Ask the children to plan and talk about a second, alternative version of the sixth chapter.

5. Picture planning

Objective
To draft a narrative, creating settings, characters and plot.

What you need
Copies of *Flat Stanley*.

Cross-curricular link
Art and design

What to do

- Hold up two books: *Charlie and the Chocolate Factory* and *Charlie and the Great Glass Elevator* by Roald Dahl. Ask: *What do the titles share?* (The name 'Charlie') *Which one should you read first?* (*Charlie and the Chocolate Factory*) Explain that one book is the sequel to the other: it continues its story.

- Return to the ending of *Flat Stanley*. Point out that Jeff Brown has left the reader with many questions. In particular, the reader wonders if Stanley will change again.

- Invite partners to share ideas for a sequel to *Flat Stanley*. Ask: *What is the problem?* (Stanley has started to change from his proper shape: perhaps he becomes flat again, or larger or string-shaped.) *How does Arthur help?* (He looks for something to change Stanley back into shape.) *What events happen because of his shape? What is the ending?*

- Talk about a story's usual structure of four chronological sections: opening, something happens, events to sort it out, ending. Give each child paper to fold into quarters and number and label with these section headings ('1. Opening', '2. Something happens' and so on.)

- Invite everyone to create a pictorial storyboard for their sequel. Each section may contain more than one picture and should show the setting, some characters and an indication of what is happening. Once completed, save them for Activity 6.

Differentiation
Support: Let partners work together on the same story. Provide ideas for one or two sections.

6. Building a story

Objective
To compose and rehearse sentences orally before writing a text.

What you need
Copies of *Flat Stanley*, photocopiable page 43 'Building a story'.

What to do

- Remind the children of the previous activity in which they planned a sequel to *Flat Stanley* on a pictorial storyboard.

- Present a pictorial storyboard that you have completed for another, unrelated story. As a storyteller, recount what is happening in each picture.

- Explain that a story planner is useful when making notes. Demonstrate writing notes to relate to your pictorial storyboard, and point out that you are writing words and phrases, not sentences. Make sure that the children recognise the difference.

- Return to the children's pictorial storyboards from the previous activity. Suggest that they use their storyboard to tell their story to a partner.

- Give out individual copies of photocopiable page 43 'Building a story'. Ask the children to write notes for their sequel.

- Finally, ask them to write their story in one or more extended writing sessions. Emphasise that they must develop their notes into complete sentences. Demonstrate converting some of your own notes into sentences. Encourage regular pauses so that the children rehearse a sentence orally before writing it.

Differentiation
Support: Let children work with their partners from the 'Picture planning' activity, writing only one or two notes for each section.

Extension: Ask children to add two time conjunctions to each section's notes.

Book review

● Use this sheet to help you write a book review for *Flat Stanley*.

Title:

_____

Author: _____

_____

_____

_____

Illustrator: _____

_____

_____

_____

Who would enjoy this story?

● _____

● _____

● _____

● _____

● _____

● _____

Describe the setting and plot.

_____

_____

_____

_____

_____

_____

My favourite part:

_____

_____

_____

_____

My least favourite part:

_____

Now give the book a rating out of five by colouring the stars.

☆ ☆ ☆ ☆ ☆

_____

_____

_____

Becoming famous

- Make notes to help you plan a Chapter 6 for *Flat Stanley*. Answer the questions to help you.

What happens the next morning?

Does the family go out?

Does Stanley feel nervous or happy?

How do the other Lambchops feel?

Do people see Stanley?

What do they think has happened?

How do people learn about Arthur's idea?

Are they surprised?

Does anyone interview Arthur?

Are his name and picture in the newspaper?

Does Arthur enjoy being famous?

How does the book end?

Other ideas I plan to include:

-
-
-
-
-

Building a story

● Use your picture storyboard to help you write planning notes for your story.

1. Opening

_____

_____

_____

_____

_____

_____

_____

_____

_____

_____

2. Something happens

_____

_____

_____

_____

_____

_____

_____

_____

_____

_____

3. Events to sort it out

_____

_____

_____

_____

_____

_____

_____

_____

_____

_____

4. Ending

_____

_____

_____

_____

_____

_____

_____

_____

_____

_____

ASSESSMENT ▶

1. A missing page

Objective
To discuss writing similar to that which they are planning to write in order to understand and learn from its structure, vocabulary and grammar.

What you need
Copies of *Flat Stanley*.

What to do
- Complete this activity after reading the third chapter.

- Examine the first half of the third chapter. Discuss the writer's style in pairs and then as a whole class. Ask: Is dialogue or narrative description used? (There is a mixture.) Read aloud some of the dialogue when the Lambchops meet Mr Lambchop's old friend. What do the children notice about the structure and punctuation? Point out the features of direct speech.

- Investigate other aspects of the writer's style: powerful verbs ('jostled', 'soaked'); detailed descriptions ('speeding taxis', 'hurrying people'); varied sentences.

- Present a scenario: a page has been lost from Jeff Brown's original manuscript. Suggest that the missing page involves another meeting on the Lambchops' journey home. Ask: *Who is the person? Is it raining? Does Stanley stay rolled up? What comments are made about Stanley? What does Arthur say?* Allow the children to discuss ideas with a partner before they write the missing page. Their writing style should be consistent with Jeff Brown's.

- Afterwards, ask the children to read their pages to one another in reading groups.

Differentiation
Support: Provide children with a writing frame of sentence openers.

2. Reading characters

Objective
To infer characters' feelings, thoughts and motives from their actions.

What you need
Copies of *Flat Stanley*.

What to do
- Remind the children of how Stanley helped his mother retrieve her ring in Chapter 2. Look at his response (he cries out 'Hooray!') and discuss any illustration of the scene in your edition. Ask: *How does helping make Stanley feel?*

- Re-read the beginning of Chapter 4 together, up to 'He told it to Mr Dart'. Discuss what Stanley wants to do (help Mr Dart to stop the thieves) and encourage the children to suggest why (because Stanley enjoys helping; because he likes to use being flat to do exciting things).

- Now ask pairs to read on until 'But I know what I like'. Encourage them to compare what Stanley thought would happen (he would dress as a cowboy) with what Mr Dart decides (Stanley will be disguised as a shepherdess). Ask them to imagine and discuss how Stanley feels about this and to look for clues in the text ('Stanley was so disgusted that he could hardly speak'; Mr Dart says 'You look fierce, not happy, Stanley'). Also consider any illustrations, looking at the different emotions displayed on people's faces and in their body language.

- Read the rest of Chapter 4 together, and then ask the children to write a few paragraphs about Stanley's thoughts and feelings in the museum scene. Ask: *Do you think he regrets helping in the end?*

Differentiation
Extension: Ask children to write about the thoughts of Mr Dart or the robbers.

3. Curing flatness

Objective
To draft and write non-narrative material, using simple organisational devices.

What you need
Copies of *Flat Stanley*.

Cross-curricular link
Computing

What to do

- Direct the children to the final part of the first chapter. Read aloud: 'Well, that's mostly how it is with these cases'. Comment that this implies that there have been other cases of flatness and Dr Dan does not know of a cure. Return to the end of the book. Suggest that the Lambchops are likely to re-visit Dr Dan to report Stanley's recovery. He will be eager to share the case with other doctors, perhaps in an article for a medical magazine.

- Display Extract 4 and point out the organisational devices common to non-fiction writing: headings, subheadings, bullet points and numbers or letters. Explain that illustrations are usually informative rather than decorative.

- Put the children in pairs to discuss what Dr Dan should include in his article. Share ideas. Agree that he would supply introductory background to Stanley's case before explaining in further paragraphs how the patient was cured.

- Ask the children to write their article, treating it as a draft that they proofread, check, correct, improve and edit. Encourage them to consider: spelling, punctuation, the wording of sentences, a formal, impersonal style and the organisation of their report.

- Allow the children to use computers to type a final version or, if preferred, the whole process from first draft to final edit could take place on the computer.

Differentiation
Support: Expect less writing and let partners talk to each other about the division of their article.

4. Discussing books

Objective
To give well-structured narratives for different purposes, including for expressing feelings.

What you need
Copies of *Flat Stanley*.

What to do

- Do this activity after finishing the book.

- Explain that you will be reading *Flat Stanley* with next year's class, that you would like your new children to know a little about the story and that information from children in this year's class would be useful. Use partner and then class discussion to share comments.

- Explain that you want the children to speak about the book, and not simply to read out what they write. Suggest that cue cards would remind them what to say next.

- Give the children a piece of paper to fold into quarters for four cue cards. Each cue card should be brief and clear in the form of notes or sketches. Provide these guidelines: card one should introduce the book (title and author); card two should pick out important story events (do illustrations contribute?); card three should describe characters (who is the most interesting?); card four should hint at how the story unfolds (what holds the reader's interest all the way through?)

- After preparing their cue cards, let the children practise their speaking with a partner. Organise listening groups, so that everyone experiences speaking to a group.

- Arrange a visit from next year's class or from other children in the year below, so that the children can tell a visiting partner about the story.

Differentiation
Support: Allow partners to work together on their cue cards and oral retelling, each speaking for some of the time.

Extension: Expect children to speak at greater length and to provide perceptive details.

5. Setting the scene

Objective
To draft and write by creating settings, characters and plot.

What you need
Copies of *Flat Stanley*.

What to do

- Direct the children to the book's opening page. Comment that Brown begins abruptly, without details of setting and characters. Ask: *How does the reader learn more?* Point out that facts are revealed gradually (the fourth chapter reveals that the Lambchops live in a flat) or the reader works them out (Mrs Lambchop is very fussy). Suggest that Brown could have written an introductory chapter.

- Ask pairs to talk about the story's setting. Share information: the Lambchops' flat is in a building with other flats; it is in a city (probably in America) with busy streets; there is a famous Museum of Art in the city. Would the children add new details? Ask them to make brief notes. Repeat the process of partner and class discussion, and note making for the characters.

- Explain that they are going to write the opening paragraphs of an introductory chapter. Let them work on a draft, composing sentences and reading them aloud to themselves and a partner. Encourage constructive feedback as partners help each other to monitor whether their writing makes sense. Ask them to write their polished paragraphs.

- Put the children into groups to read their writing aloud to one another. Remind them to consider their tone, intonation and volume so that their meaning is clear. Invite children to read their work to the class.

Differentiation
Support: Expect just one paragraph and let them read it aloud to you before they write.

Extension: Ask the children to write further paragraphs in their introductory chapter.

6. Brotherly love

Objective
To identify themes in a wide range of books.

What you need
Copies of *Flat Stanley*, photocopiable page 47 'Brotherly love'.

What to do

- Draw attention to: '"Thank you, Arthur," Stanley said. "Thank you very much"' and 'The brothers were shaking hands' in the final chapter. Suggest that the brothers' close relationship is a major theme of this book. Briefly discuss other books children have read where sibling relationships are a theme.

- Direct the children to the point in the second chapter when Arthur tries to slide under a door and to his attempt in the third chapter to flatten himself with a pile of books. Ask: *Why does he do these things? What gives him the ideas?* Do the children agree with Mr and Mrs Lambchop's opinion that Arthur is jealous of Stanley?

- Point out that during the story, Stanley becomes unhappy. Ask: *What changes to make him unhappy?* (People call him names.) *How does Arthur discover Stanley's sadness?* (In the fifth chapter, he hears Stanley crying.)

- Direct the children to the fifth chapter and discuss the honest conversation that the boys have. Point out that Arthur calls Stanley 'brave'. Read aloud the paragraph in which Arthur 'took hold of Stanley's hand'. Ask: *What is emphasised?* (The boys need each other.)

- Give out individual copies of photocopiable page 47 'Brotherly love'. Explain the headings and encourage partner discussion before independent writing of polished sentences.

Differentiation
Support: Accept simple explanations and more general reference to the text.

Extension: Expect a more detailed answer with closer reference to the text; ask children to identify a similar theme in other books they have read, and compare them.

Brotherly love

● Discuss each event with your partner before writing sentences.

The problem	How brotherly love is shown	The effect
Arthur is jealous (Chapter 3)		
Stanley is crying (Chapter 5)		
Stanley wants to change back (Chapter 5)		

SCHOLASTIC

READ & RESPOND

Available in this series:

978-1407-15879-2

978-1407-14224-1

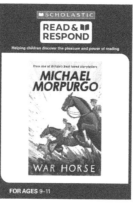

978-1407-16063-4

978-1407-16056-6

978-1407-14228-9

978-1407-16069-6

978-1407-16070-2

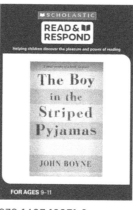

978-1407-16071-9

978-1407-14230-2

978-1407-16057-3

978-1407-16064-1

978-1407-14223-4

978-0702-30890-1

978-0702-30859-8

To find out more,
visit www.scholastic.co.uk/read-and-respond